■SCHOLASTIC
News
Nonfiction Read

What Is the Statue of Liberty?

By Janice Behrens

Children's Press®
An Imprint of Scholastic Inc.
New York Toronto London Auckland Sydney
Mexico City New Delhi Hong Kong
Danbury, Connecticut

These content vocabulary word builders are for grades 1–2.

Subject Consultant: Eli J. Lesser, MA, Director of Education, National Constitution Center, Philadelphia, Pennsylvania

Reading Consultant: Cecilia Minden-Cupp, PhD, Early Literacy Consultant and Author, Chapel Hill, North Carolina

Photographs © 2009: Alamy Images: 4 bottom left, 8 (Peter Barritt), 19 bottom right (Jeff Greenberg), 23 top left (Jim Havey), 23 bottom right (Hisham Ibrahim/Photov.com), 19 top center (LHB Photo), 23 bottom left (Jason Lindsey), 19 bottom left (David Morris), 23 top right (Visions of America, LLC); Corbis Images: 11 (Edwin Levick/The Mariners' Museum), 4 bottom right, 6 (Bill Ross); Digital Railroad: cover (Suki Coughlin/Mira), 20, 21 main (Rob Crandall/Stock Connection), 7 (Dallas and John Heaton/Stock Connection); Getty Images: back cover, 2, 9 (Frans Lemmens), 19 center left, 19 center right (Erin Patrice O'Brien), 19 top right (Scott Olson), 19 top left (Melanie Stetson Freeman/The Christian Science Monitor); JupiterImages: 15 main; Lee W. Nelson, www.inetours.com: 15 inset; Library of Congress: 13 bottom; Photolibrary: 5 top left, 16 (Index Stock Imagery), 1, 5 bottom left, 10 (PureStock); Redux Pictures: 5 bottom right, 18 (Ozier Muhammad/The New York Times), 17 main (Ruby Washington/The New York Times); Statue of Liberty National Monument/National Park Service: 17 inset (American Museum of Immigration), 21 inset; The Granger Collection, New York: 13 top; The Image Works/Nancy Richmond: 4 top, 14. Maps by James McMahon

Original Book Design: Simonsays Design!
Art Direction, Production, and Digital Imaging: Scholastic Classroom Magazines

Library of Congress Cataloging-in-Publication Data

Behrens, Janice, 1972-
What Is the Statue of Liberty? / Janice Behrens.
   p. cm. – (Scholastic news nonfiction readers)
Includes bibliographical references and index.
ISBN 13: 978-0-531-21091-8 (lib. bdg.)   978-0-531-22428-1 (pbk.)
ISBN 10: 0-531-21091-X (lib. bdg.)   0-531-22428-7 (pbk.)
1. Statue of Liberty (New York, N.Y.)–Juvenile literature. 2. Statue of Liberty National Monument (N.Y. and N.J.)–Juvenile literature. 3. New York (N.Y.)–Buildings, structures, etc.–Juvenile literature. I. Title. II. Series.
F128.64.L6B43 2008
974.7'1–dc22   2008025433

CONTENTS

Word Hunt 4–5

What Is the Statue of Liberty? 6–7

Liberty Island 8–9

In Search of Freedom 10–11

A Gift from France 12–13

Why Is She Green? 14–15

Inside the Statue 16–17

Visiting the Statue 18–19

A Look at Lady Liberty 20–21

Your New Words 22

More Famous American Statues 23

Index 24

Find Out More 24

Meet the Author 24

WORD HUNT

Look for these words as you read. They will be in **bold**.

copper
(**kop**-ur)

island
(**eye**-luhnd)

statue
(**stach**-oo)

4

crown
(kroun)

France
(franss)

torch
(torch)

visitors
(**vi**-zit-urz)

5

What Is the Statue of Liberty?

The **Statue** of Liberty is one of the tallest statues on Earth! People call the statue Lady Liberty. Liberty means freedom. She stands for freedom.

statue

Lady Liberty stands on Liberty **Island**. The island is near New York City.

She has stood there for over 120 years.

island

Liberty Island is in the Hudson River, between New York and New Jersey.

Long ago, many people came to America by boat. They came from all over the world. They came to live in freedom.

The Statue of Liberty held her **torch** high to greet them.

torch

The Statue of Liberty was the first thing many people saw when coming to America.

The statue was not always on Liberty Island. She was built in **France**. She was a gift from the French people.

How did she get to the U.S.? First, they took her apart. Then, they packed her in 214 boxes!

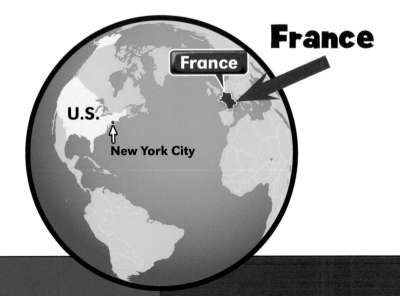

France

It took workers nine years to build the Statue of Liberty.

Lady Liberty's skin is made of **copper**. The sun and air have turned her green over the years. When she was new, she was brown, like a copper penny.

copper

This copy of the statue's face shows what it looked like when it was new.

Inside are iron bars. They hold her up, just like your bones hold you up.

There are stairs inside too. There are 142 steps from her feet to her **crown**!

crown

This is what you see inside the Statue of Liberty.

Millions of **visitors** come to see the Statue of Liberty each year. They take a boat, just like people did long ago.

Lady Liberty still stands tall to greet them.

visitors

A LOOK AT LADY LIBERTY

The crown has seven spikes. They stand for the seven continents and seven seas.

Her nose is about as long as a nine-year-old child is tall.

Her skin is only as thick as two pennies put together.

The flame of the torch is covered in gold.

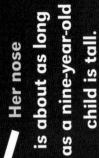

The book in her hand has the date July 4, 1776. That is the birthday of the United States of America.

Some people say the statue looks like the artist's mother. This is a picture of his mother. What do you think?

The artist who designed the Statue of Liberty was named Frederic-Auguste Bartholdi (FREH-duh-reek oh-GOOST Bar-TOL-dee).

YOUR NEW WORDS

copper (**kop**-ur) a reddish brown metal

crown (kroun) something a king or queen wears on his or her head

France (franss) the largest country in Western Europe

island (**eye**-luhnd) a piece of land surrounded by water

statue (**stach**-oo) a model of a person, animal, or thing

torch (torch) a flaming light that can be carried in the hand

visitors (**vi**-zit-urz) people that go to see a place or other people